SCOUT&JET
THE ADVENTURE BEGINS

Theophany Eystathioy

Illustrated by:
Lisa Thompson

Edited by:
Cheri Hanson

A Little PhDs Book
www.littlephds.com

A Little PhDs Book
www.littlephds.com

Copyright 2016 – Little PhDs, All Rights Reserved

Library & Archives Canada Cataloging – in –Publication Data
Eystathioy, Theophany
Scout and Jet: The Adventure Begins/ written by Theophany Eystathioy ; illustrated by Lisa Thompson

Summary: Follow the adventures of Scout and Jet, who travel back in time to meet real historical figures whose discoveries advanced our scientific knowledge. In this book, the kids meet Mary Anning – one of the world's youngest scientists, who made enormous contributions to the field of paleontology, and to science at large.
– Provided by publisher

ISBN 978-0-9952552-1-0 (ebook)
ISBN 978-0-9952552-0-3 (pbk)

To my children, never stop dreaming.

-T.E

"It will be an adventure," Jet's mom said with a smile. "I promise." So far this trip was boring. They had driven for what seemed like hours. Scout hadn't even looked at her mom. She was still mad that they couldn't bring their tablet along. They had exited the main highway and were entering narrow dirt roads surrounded by forest. Around the bend, Scout and Jet saw a strange-looking cottage.

"We're here!" said their father as he pulled up to the curb. Scout looked out the window. An older woman stood in front of the cottage, her dress blowing gently in the breeze. The cottage behind her looked odd and old and worn down. Big stone steps from the left and the right led to a wooden front door, topped with an arch. Green vines and tree branches wrapped around the cottage like tentacles.

"Now remember your manners," their mother said, looking back at both children with a stern warning. Scout and Jet got out of the car and reluctantly followed their parents up the stairs.

"Hello Scout and Jet," the older lady beamed. "You can call me Charm. Welcome to my home." She waved her hand and gestured to the cottage behind them. Not only were they in the middle of nowhere, but the cottage seemed eerie. The kids watched as their parents and Charm ducked slightly to enter the door. Jet and Scout looked at each other. They got on their tippy toes and the tops of their heads almost, *almost,* reached the peak of the door arch. As they entered the cottage, they noticed it was roomier. At least there was more headspace. They were surprised. The cottage looked so small from the outside.

Charm smiled at the children. She peered at them over the rim of her glasses. Her silver hair was pulled into a bun.

"You will have to share a room. Go up the stairs to your right," she continued, "and you're free to roam the cottage as you wish." The wooden stairs creaked with every step Jet and Scout took. When they got to their room, it was really small. *Great*, Scout thought. Things couldn't be more perfect. Now she had to share a room with her brother! Two single beds were crammed into the room, which had an old fireplace and a small window lined with lace curtains.

Scout sighed. She was tired and frustrated. She turned to Jet: "Did you see a TV?" Before Jet could reply, Charm answered from the doorway. "Oh I don't have a TV or a computer here. There is no Wi-Fi."

Jet's mouth dropped open. Scout looked stunned. How could Mom and Dad have forgotten to mention that?

Charm didn't seem to notice. "Dinner will be ready in about an hour. I hope you like fried frog legs and snails baked in butter." Scout thought she saw a smirk on Charm's face. Whatever the case, Scout was certainly not laughing not about the Wi-Fi situation, nor the dinner menu.

It was dark now, and the moonlight beamed through their bedroom window. Everyone was in bed. Scout and Jet could hear their parents snoring, and unfortunately, they were not in sync.

"Scout? Are you awake?" Jet didn't wait for a response. "I can't sleep."

"Me, neither."

"So what are we supposed to do?" Jet whispered. "I'm so bored. I don't care that there are forests around here. Forests are boring. This place is soooo boring."

Scout sighed. "And we're stuck here for two weeks. I miss my friends. I miss the TV. I miss my computer. I want my tablet!" All they could do was stare at the ceiling. Besides the snoring, the kids could hear the old house shifting. Everything just seemed to creak and groan.

Jet got up from his bed. Scout could see his silhouette in the moonlight. "It's the middle of the night, Jet. We are not supposed to be up!" She took her older sister role very seriously.

Jet ignored her and headed for the bedroom door.

"Fine. I'm coming too." Scout's feet touched the cold, wooden floor.

Creak! That sound was getting annoying. It was also kind of spooky.

"Wait for me," Scout said in a louder whisper, before running right into a table sitting in the middle of the hallway. "Ouch!" Then she heard a *clunk*.

"Shhhh," Jet hissed.

"I know!" Scout snapped. *That hurt*, she thought, and touched her leg. Something had fallen off the table. Jet was already reaching for it.

"A flashlight!" Jet turned it on and Scout walked beside him. What good luck! This would keep them from running into more furniture.

They headed down the narrow staircase. It was a good thing that they hadn't woken anyone up. Scout's stomach growled and she veered towards the kitchen.

"Shhh," she said to Jet. "Be quiet. Grab an apple if you want." *Fine*, Jet thought to himself. The cookies he remembered seeing were no longer on the counter. He found the light switch, but it didn't work. Nothing happened.

"That's strange," Scout said, peering out from behind him. "I guess it doesn't matter. We can see okay." They could see much better now, as their eyes had adjusted to the dark. In fact, the downstairs didn't seem so shadowy anymore. Moonlight was pouring through the small windows. Both Scout and Jet felt a little spooked, but neither would say so. It was a matter of pride.

As they turned to leave, something caught their eyes. Towards the back of the kitchen, down the short hallway, they could see a small door.

"What's that?" Scout asked Jet. How come she hadn't noticed it before? Jet was already down the hall, his flashlight dancing over the door.

Scout's hand touched the doorknob. "It's locked."

"Let me see," Jet passed the flashlight to Scout. Jet reefed on the doorknob and shook the door as quietly as possible.

Creak…

The door opened. The kids just stood there, their eyes wide with surprise. One moment, then two went by.

"Let's go in." Scout tugged on Jet's sleeve, dragging him behind her. She searched the wall for a light switch. Nothing. Come to think of it, there was no furniture, and no lamps or chandelier. The room was dark, except for the moon shining in through a large window. The lace curtains had been pulled back. There was enough light to see bookshelves lining the walls. There were so many books, stretching from floor to ceiling, and from wall to wall.

"Holy guacamole, look at all these books!" Scout dusted off a few spines with her pajama sleeve. "What are all of these?"

Ah-choo…!

Jet sneezed loudly. "It's so dusty! Look at all of the cobwebs." Jet wiped his nose with his arm. Scout's flashlight bounced on the books.

"Come on," said Jet. This is boring. Let's just go back." He turned to leave. Scout began to follow.

THUMP!....

Jet and Scout screamed – and then clasped their hands over their mouths. They waited for their parents to come stomping down the stairs. But luckily (or unluckily) no one came.

"What was that?" Scout had already jumped back to the doorway. She was ready to flee, until she noticed something on the floor. It was a book lying partly open. Jet walked over for a closer look: "Give me that flashlight."

"Say please," Scout scolded. But Jet grabbed the flashlight from her hand. Before Scout could complain, she saw where Jet was shining the light. The book was open to a printed page. Scout read aloud.

Are you ready for an adventure? Want to take a ride? Come with me and we will go back in time...

Jet looked at Scout.

Jet gulped and finished the sentence.

"Come and meet Mary Anning..."

strong gust of wind knocked Jet down.

He looked up and grabbed his sister's arm. Jet could see the blue sky. It was daytime and they were no longer at the cottage.

Ahhh!

Both kids yelled in unison. They couldn't get a stable foothold. Their feet were sliding out from underneath them and they tried desperately to regain their balance. Scout grabbed Jet and pulled him down. They were now sitting on the side of a cliff, trying to catch their breath. A moment, then two, passed silently.

"Where are we?" Jet looked around. "Where is the cottage?"

"I don't know, Dorothy, but we are not in Kansas anymore," Scout replied.

"Did you hit your head? I am your b…r…o…t… h…e…r," Jet said slowly, looking hypnotically into her eyes.

"No, I mean… oh, never mind." Scout was puzzled. They were on a cliff. There was no one around. Certainly not her parents or Charm. As she tried to focus, she could feel the sun on her face. It was a warm day. She could hear waves crashing and realized the ocean was below them.

"This is definitely worse than my regular nightmare," said Jet. "You know, the one where pickles are chasing me. But I always fight them with my gigantic super soakers. And I always win." Jet smiled.

Scout ignored her brother. "Maybe she knows what's going on."

"Who?" Jet asked, following Scout's pointing finger.

There was a girl in the distance. Scout couldn't be completely sure, but she seemed to be about their age. *She must have lost something,* Scout thought, because it looked like she was searching the ground.

"Let's go," said Scout. They slowly made their way down the cliff, zigzagging to stay balanced on the steep slope. They walked up to the girl on the beach.

"Excuse me," said Jet. "We're lost and need some help."

The girl was dressed strangely. Granted, Scout and Jet were in their pajamas, but this girl was wearing a weird hat and a really long, grey dress. The girl got up from a crouching position and shielded her eyes from the sun.

"That happens," she said. "You need to watch where you are stepping. One second you are on flat, even land and the next thing you know, you could be sliding down the cliff. You have to be careful." She looked away, staring into the distance. "My dad fell of these cliffs. He died after that."

Scout listened intently. Maybe this girl could tell them where they were. She felt sad, too, for what the girl had said about her dad. "I'm sorry," Scout said, remembering her manners. "Umm, do you have a cell phone? We really need to call our parents."

The girl crouched down again, looking intently at some big rocks. She rose and squinted at Scout. "I am sorry. I do not understand what you mean."

Jet noticed that she had a strange accent.

Scout also noticed that the girl's face flushed a little. "I do not go to school. My family cannot send me." She looked back at them. "I do know how to read and write, though. I learned this at Sunday school." Before Scout could ask more questions, the girl started walking toward the cliffs.

Scout and Jet quickly caught up to her.

"I am usually here all alone. Are you looking for curiosities, too?"

"Curiosities?" Scout and Jet asked in unison.

"My dad taught me. Curiosities. That's what I am looking for. Although other people call them snake stones, or Devil's fingers. Some people are scared of them because they do not know where they came from. But not me. I find curiosities fascinating. And I make money selling them. I also find and sell shells. We need the money." The girl said the last sentence so quietly that Jet almost missed it. She sighed and tugged on her bonnet. Her brown eyes seemed to be scanning Jet and Scout.

"I am sorry. I did not introduce myself. My name is Mary Anning."

Both kids snapped to attention and looked at each other.

"Are you new here?" Mary asked. "I have never seen you before." She looked at them curiously.

Before Jet could say anything, Scout jumped in. "Yes, we are new here. My name is Scout and this is my brother, Jet."

"You must be from someplace else. Your clothing is unusual." Mary turned and continued walking. Jet grabbed Scout's arm.

"Mary Anning," he said quietly, "as in the book we started reading…"

Scout nodded slowly.

"I don't get it."

"Neither do I. Let's keep talking to her." Scout turned to their new friend. "Mary! Wait up."

The three kids walked side by side. A gentle breeze was coming from the ocean. It felt cool on their skin, because the sun was so hot. "We need to be careful, because these cliffs become unstable after a rainfall. Landslides can happen easily." Mary's eyes darted up and down the cliff.

She turned to Scout and Jet. "It's nice to have some company. My brother joins me sometimes. But mostly it is just me out here." Biting her lower lip, Mary clenched at her dress. She looked at them intently. "Can you keep a secret?" Before they could answer, Mary kept talking. "I want to show you something." There was a gleam in her eyes as she smiled. Scout thought she looked really happy.

"We can keep a secret," Scout said, looking at her brother. "At least some of us can."

Jet ignored her. He looked around. There were huge rocks and boulders everywhere. Why was Mary here? She wasn't going swimming. Why was she looking at these boring rocks?

"Here it is. My brother and I found this." Mary pointed to something sticking out of a rock beside the cliff. Scout peered down and yawned. They needed to find their parents. Scout thought they should politely excuse themselves and go. Jet was also getting tired. Looking at rocks and cliffs wasn't exactly thrilling.

Mary must have seen the blank looks on their faces. "I know it doesn't seem like much. You need to look at this carefully. My dad taught me. See here." She crouched down again. "This is not an ordinary piece of rock. Look. The exposed part is a skull. I have started to chisel it out." Mary pointed with her index finger. Jet and Scout looked closer; there was a pattern in the rock. Mary's voice went higher and she waved her hands in excitement. "I have also found the rest of it. The skeleton is here."

When Scout and Jet crouched down beside Mary, they could see the pattern. Holy guacamole! There was a skull and what looked like a skeleton in the rock. Scout gasped. Jet blinked slowly. They both ran their hands over it.

It dawned on them.

Scout and Jet looked at one another and then at Mary.

"Fossils!" Scout whispered to Jet. Her brother nodded. "Fossils are the remains of ancient creatures. Animals that died a long time ago and were buried in the earth." Scout suddenly remembered what she had learned in school.

"Right. They are fossils," Jet said softly. "But Mary calls them curiosities."

Mary, unaware of their quiet conversation, stood up to join them. "My brother thinks it's a crocodile skull," she said. "But I think it's something else. I think it's from a creature that died long, long ago. If you ask me, I think the world was once a very different place. And I think the world is really old."

The words "long ago" triggered something in Jet's memory. *Long ago….* The book at the cottage said: *we will go back in time.* Oh no! So when was now?

"Um, what year is this?" Jet took a breath and held it in.

"It's 1811, of course." Mary looked at him with a puzzled expression.

Scout and Jet stared back at her. The year 1811 was over 200 years ago.

"I will get the rest of this out of the rock and I will sell it," Mary said, wiping the sweat off her forehead. "This place is full of curiosities. I love looking for them. These curiosities tell a story – a story about our past. I just know it." Mary looked off into the distance. "I even draw what I find. I like to keep records." She beamed with pride. "I will find more. I am sure of it. And the money I earn from selling these will help my family."

Scout really wanted Mary to succeed. She was doing something important. "Good luck, Mary."

CHAPTER 4

Suddenly, the kids felt a strong gust of wind. The blue sky grew dark.

Whoosh… Jet grabbed Scout's arm – hard.

"Ouch! That hurts!" Scout slapped Jet's hand away and looked around. It was dark. Moonlight flooded in from the window. They were in the cottage again.

"We're back." Jet said, happily. They both looked around, blinking, before glancing down at the open book on the floor. They were still sitting in the same position.

Jet paused and took a breath. His flashlight was still pointing at the book, illuminating just five words printed on the page.

How old is the earth?

"Huh?" Jet scratched his head. This was weird. "I don't know," he said aloud.

Scout looked sideways at Jet and grabbed the book. She quickly flipped through the pages as though looking for an answer. "That's it?"

"What do you mean, that's it?" Jet grabbed the book from her hands and examined the remaining pages. They were all blank.

"What a strange question – and what a weird way to end the book." Scout said.

"How old is the earth?" said Jet. "What does that have to do with Mary Anning?"

"Well… maybe there are clues in the fossil Mary found. Hmmm. How old do you think the world is?" Scout asked her brother.

"I don't know. Ten thousand, or maybe a million?" Jet said breathlessly.

"A million? Yeah, right!" Scout mocked. "It must be more like 10 million."

Not to be outdone, Jet jumped in: "How about one hundred million?" Before Scout and Jet could keep bantering, they jumped in surprise. The flashlight shook, but Jet kept it focused on the book. Words began to appear on the blank page:

About 4.5 billion years old.

"I… the paper… the words." Jet stuttered as he stared at the book. He regained his composure and finished his thought. "Wasn't that page blank?"

"Yes," Scout replied quietly.

"Well, I guess we were way off." Jet cleared his throat and spoke louder, trying to shake off his fear.

Scout crouched over the book, took a deep breath and picked it up again. All the other pages were blank.

Jet had an idea. "Scout. Ask a question!"

Scout set the book back down and backed away. "Okay," she said. Her mind raced. She knew now that the world was really old and she knew that fossils were old, too. *Here goes nothing,* she thought. "How old was the fossil that Mary found?" Scout asked, barely in a whisper.

Words began appearing, one at a time.

It was 200 million years old.

Holy hummus! Jet and Scout looked at one another. Jet was feeling brave. It was only a book, after all. Okay – a magic book and they were sitting in a dark room. It was kind of spooky. Jet glanced at Scout. She wasn't leaving, and Jet didn't want to go either. Not just yet. The book was only a book, but then again, hadn't they just landed on a cliff? In 1811? Jet eyed the book with suspicion. He still had questions. But to be safe, he would keep his distance. Jet really wanted to know more about Mary's "curiosity."

He cleared his throat. "What was the fossil that Mary found?"

Jet and Scout waited.

It was a sea creature, called an Ichthyosaurus.

"Ich… thy...o … saurus…" Jet said slowly, trying to pronounce the long word.

Yes. It means "fish lizard."

The kids looked at each other with surprise. The words began to emerge faster, and they kept on coming.

The cliffs and beach where Mary searched for fossils used to be the bottom of the ocean. Hundreds of millions of years ago, the area you explored was all under water. Mary uncovered fossils from strange sea creatures that no longer exist. When these sea creatures died, they were buried in the ocean floor. The waters eventually receded and the fossils were there, waiting to be discovered.

Scout moved closer to the book, mesmerized. She spoke quietly: "Did Mary find other fossils?"

Yes. Several years later, she found a plesiosaurus, which is another sea creature. She also found a flying creature called a pterodactylus.

Scout's mind was racing.

"I wonder what it looked like back then. I mean, a couple hundred million years ago at the beach, where Mary was looking." Scout stared intently at the book.

Jet watched as the page flipped, revealing a strange drawing. Words began to appear below the picture.

This is what the sea looked like in ancient Dorset, England. That's where Mary lived, too, hundreds of millions of years later. This artwork was created in 1830 by geologist Henry de la Beche. His drawing was based on Mary Anning's discoveries.

"Wow! What are these creatures?" Jet wondered aloud.

Pterodactylus flies in the sky and an Icthyosaurus has grabbed a Plesiosaurus by the neck.

"Amazing!" Scout said as she pointed at the different sea creatures.

Jet studied the picture closely. "Was Mary a scientist?"

Not in the traditional way. Mary did not have a degree in science. But she was a scientist. She was curious, and she asked questions. She observed and noticed things that others ignored or did not see.

"Really?" Jet said, mostly to himself.

Yes. When Mary was little, schools didn't teach kids about fossils. They didn't know what was buried in the earth. With the help of Mary's discoveries, scientists learned how the world began. They were eager to talk to her and to see her fossils. Mary influenced many scientists.

"But how could she do that?" asked Scout. "She was just a kid!"

Yes. But she was observant and curious. She was creative. Isn't it amazing that she dug up a 200-million-year-old sea creature when she was 12 years old?

"Yes, it is!" Scout agreed. "How come we haven't heard about Mary Anning before?"

You have. Do you know the line, 'She sells sea shells by the sea shore?'

Jet looked at Scout. "We know that one."

Some people say it's based on Mary Anning's life. This famous tongue twister was written in 1908 by Terry Sullivan.

"I wish we could go back and see more fossils." Jet said, sighing.

You can. You can go today. There are museums that display the fossils Mary found in the 1800s.

"Cool!" Scout and Jet said at the same time. Both kids were lost with their thoughts. Time passed. They waited to see if more words would appear on the pages. Nothing happened.

The room was getting brighter. They glanced at the window and saw that the sun was coming up. Jet turned off the flashlight.

They had been down here a long time. But they weren't ready to go just yet.

"Mary Anning changed science." Scout said, breaking the silence.

"And we got to meet her," Jet added. "That is so cool."

Scout gently closed the book and put it back in an empty spot, now visible on the shelf. Suddenly, they both felt tired. Alone with their own thoughts they quietly tiptoed upstairs and went to bed.

"Good morning, you two!" their father said cheerily. "Where are you running off to in such a hurry?"

Scout and Jet dashed toward the back door of the cottage.

Scout looked at her bucket, spoon and trowel. She glanced up again and saw Charm grinning.

"We're going to look for fossils!" Jet said before Scout could answer.

"Have fun, kids," Charm said, winking. "Life sure is an adventure."

SCOUT&JET

SCOUT&JET
THE ADVENTURE BEGINS

COMING SOON:

INTO THE GOBI DESERT

INTO EGYPT

A Little PhDs Book
www.littlephds.com

ABOUT THE AUTHOR

Theophany Eystathioy has a PhD and has worked extensively in the field of cellular and molecular biology. Formerly an adjunct professor at the University of Calgary and a technology analyst in intellectual property, Theophany lives with her husband and her two children. Her goal is to share the fun and curiosity of science with kids of all ages, while fostering a lifelong love of this fascinating subject.

www.ingramcontent.com/pod-product-compliance
Lightning Source LLC
Chambersburg PA
CBHW050019040726
47599CB00014B/1466